A STEP-BY-STEP BOOK ABOUT
SETTING UP
A MARINE AQUARIUM

DR. C.W. EMMENS

Photography: Dr. Gerald Allen, Dr. Herbert R. Axelrod, Charles Arneson, John Burleson, Dr. Patrick Colin, Michael Gilroy, J. Kelly Giwojna, J. Kaden, Burkhard Kahl, Aaron Norman, Fred Rosenzweig, Dr. Shen, George Smit, Roger Steene, Dr. D. Terver, courtesy Nancy Aquarium.

Humorous drawings by Andrew Prendimano.

© Copyright 1990 by T.F.H. Publications, Inc.

Distributed in the UNITED STATES by T.F.H. Publications, Inc., One T.F.H. Plaza, Neptune City, NJ 07753; in CANADA to the Pet Trade by H & L Pet Supplies Inc., 27 Kingston Crescent, Kitchener, Ontario N2B 2T6; Rolf C. Hagen Ltd., 3225 Sartelon Street, Montreal 382 Quebec; in CANADA to the Book Trade by Macmillan of Canada (A Division of Canada Publishing Corporation), 164 Commander Boulevard, Agincourt, Ontario M1S 3C7; in ENGLAND by T.F.H. Publications Limited, Cliveden House/Priors Way/Bray, Maidenhead, Berkshire SL6 2HP, England; in AUSTRALIA AND THE SOUTH PACIFIC by T.F.H. (Australia) Pty. Ltd., Box 149, Brookvale 2100 N.S.W., Australia; in NEW ZEALAND by Ross Haines & Son, Ltd., 82 D Elizabeth Knox Place, Panmure, Auckland, New Zealand; in the PHILIPPINES by Bio-Research, 5 Lippay Street, San Lorenzo Village, Makati Rizal; in SOUTH AFRICA by Multipet Pty. Ltd., Box 235 New Germany, South Africa 3620. Published by T.F.H. Publications, Inc. Manufactured in the United States of America by T.F.H. Publications, Inc.

CONTENTS

THE TANK

Generally speaking, the successful home keeping of marine fishes and invertebrates has depended on modern technology. The older aquarists interested in marines tended to keep individual specimens or small communities in jars and small all-glass vessels of one kind or another. Attempts to manage larger aquaria were unsuccessful for various reasons, prominently contamination from putty and metals. Marine aquaria were managed, if at all, much the same as freshwater aquaria until it was gradually recognized that they need a very different type of management and equipment. Much of what has been gained from the development of the modern spectrum of successful methods of marine aquarium keeping has been adopted by freshwater aquarists, as an advantage in many cases, but not as a necessity.

What have been the steps enabling us to keep marine creatures as readily as they can be kept today? More or less in historical order, although very recent history, they were: adequate aeration techniques, the development of synthetic sea water, the use of all-glass tanks with silicone rubber cements, adequate filtration methods, in particular biological filtration (sewage farms in miniature), and the development of efficient and rapid transport of exotic specimens. Perhaps I should add to the list the availability of suitable foods—that has certainly helped a great deal—and the successful treatment of some of the more common diseases of marine fishes.

Facing Page: The beauty of the flourishing aquarium has attracted the hand of many a fancier to marine-life cultivation.

THE AQUARIUM

Sea water aquaria should be reasonably large, as they cannot be crowded with fishes to anything like the extent of freshwater ones. A large tank is also more stable in the constitution and temperature of the water than smaller ones, often a more important factor than in a freshwater tank. What is large? Something over 25 or 30 gallons (100–120 liters), preferably around 50 gallons (200 liters). A tank 36" x 16" x 20" (90 x 40 x 50 cm; length x width x height) is a good compromise between the biologically desirable shallow tank and the more esthetic "high" tank that shows its contents much better. A shallow tank is good because the water surface is where oxygen enters and carbon dioxide leaves, but there are ways of dealing with that problem. The 36" (90 cm) tank just cited would hold just under 50 gallons (200 liters) if filled solely with water, but if we allow for gravel, rocks, airspace, etc., 40 gallons (160 liters) is a more realistic figure. The gallon capacity is calculated by multiplying the three dimensions together and dividing by 231, which can be converted to liters by multiplying by 3.8, or, approximately, by 4.

The systems employed by marine hobbyists are as varied as the colors of the fish they maintain.

Many corals, sponges, and anemones have requirements that are more demanding than those of many fishes. Before setting up the aquarium, know which life forms will inhabit your marine system.

A tank of the size contemplated should be of new ¼" (6 mm) plate; if any larger, of ⅜" (9 mm) plate, and should have a brace across the center top 3–6" (7½–15 cm) wide. Cover glasses need to be of stout glass but not necessarily plate. They should rest on counter-sunk supports that leave them about ½" (1 cm) below the top of the tank. This prevents any overflow or salt creep. The tank must be evenly supported on a resilient sheet of styrofoam or such to take up any slight irregularities. Tape this in position before lowering the tank onto it, or it may slip about. Make sure that this support is dead level, as any slight departure will result in an ugly-looking slant to the water line.

7

LIGHTING

Don't place the aquarium where it gets much daylight, in particular direct sunlight, or it may overheat. Lighting is provided by a fluorescent tube or tubes with a reflecting hood. If you are only interested in fishes, a single tube of any type offered may be used. Some give a natural type of light, others are designed to enhance colors—it's up to you. If you want to grow higher algae (seaweeds) and not just encrusting or hair algae, more light is needed, and it must provide sufficient intensity for the algae from the two ends of the visible spectrum—red and blue. Two or three tubes will be needed, and a mixture of white and Gro-lux type tubes is best, but white light alone will do. The same is true with many anemones and corals that depend on indwelling algae for their health and much of their food. Talk to your supplier about this problem. He should be able to help.

The light should be on for at least 12 hours per day and should not be switched on or off suddenly in a darkened room. Use daylight, the room lights or a dimmer switch to avoid this and give the fishes a chance to wake up or settle down. Also, keep to a routine to which they and the invertebrates can become accustomed.

Fluorescent, incandescent, metal halide, and others: lighting selection for your marine tank depends largely on your choice of marine inhabitants.

The Tank

Heating units come in a wide assortment of styles and powers. Though employing a heater that looks good in your tank is a consideration, the wattage appropriate to the total gallons is most important.

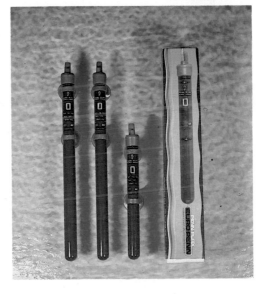

HEATING

Buy a heater-thermostat combination with external control of temperature, preferably one that is totally submersible and guaranteed suitable for salt water. A heater lying at the bottom of the tank is more efficient and less obtrusive than an upright one, but make certain that it is never covered by gravel. Too powerful a heater will cook your fishes if it sticks in the "on" position. For a 20–30 gallon (80–120 liter) tank, use a 100-watt heater; for 40–50 gallons (160–200 liters), use 150 watts; and for 60–80 gallons (240–320 liters), 200 watts. Only increase the recommended wattage if the aquarium is to be exposed to a really cold room for any length of time, below about 50°F (10°C).

Your thermometer should not contain mercury, which can poison the water if it breaks, so buy an alcohol or liquid crystal type and check it against a known accurate one. Your tropical marine tank will need a temperature in the range 77°–83°F (25°–28°C) but can be somewhat lower for many fish-only displays.

Canister filters typically pack large quantities of filtering media that effectively keep your water clean and clear. Canister filters can be used in conjunction with other filter types, i.e., undergravel, outside box, and internal power filters. Remember that all filters require regular maintenance and inspection and that no filter is a guarantee of success in the marine hobby.

AERATION

Normally the sea is heavily aerated near the surface and near its edge, and the creatures inhabiting it are accustomed to this. So aeration in a marine tank is a must and its purpose is to keep the water moving and exchanging gases with the air. This occurs at the surface, not much between the bubbles and the water unless these are very dense. Aeration is often combined with filtration, but most aquarists provide airstones to add to the effects of the filter or filters. They may or may not be really needed, depending on circumstances, but people seem to like to see bubbles rising.

Airstones come in all shapes and sizes, but what is most important is that they give medium-sized bubbles, between ⅟₃₀″ and ⅟₅₀″ (1 mm and ½mm) in diameter, as these move the water most efficiently. Very fine bubbles are O.K. in a tube, but form a mist in open water. A good brand of diaphragm pump with a volume control is all that is needed to service both airstones and filters, together with gang valves and soft airlines. Also, buy a non-return valve so that water cannot syphon back from the aquarium even if you place the pump below it.

FILTRATION

Efficient filtration is mandatory in a marine aquarium. Filters, however, do many different things. They serve to:

1. Remove particles from the water and keep it clear. Power filters (with a motor) can even remove algae and bacteria. This is a mechanical action.
2. Remove toxins and color, regulate pH (the acidity or alkalinity of the water) or remove medicines after they have done their job. This is a chemical action and is exerted by substances like activated carbon.
3. Inactivate toxins, particularly ammonia, by a biological action dependent upon the presence of the right sort of bacteria. This action only develops after some weeks or months and is not seen in filters that are replaced frequently.

Regular cleaning and water changes are vital to the good health of the marine aquarium. Many aquarists make use of powerful power filters to clean their tanks and change and polish their water. These highpower filters are available at pet shops and range in strength and price to fill your needs.

All three types of activity can best be achieved in a simple fashion by combining the actions of a carbon filter and an undergravel filter. A carbon filter uses a sandwich of activated carbon or charcoal between two filter mats. The mats filter mechanically, but they are there principally because the carbon must be of a fine, dull granular type and needs retaining. Shiny large "coals" are useless. Only a few ounces (100 or 200 g) of fine carbon are needed for a medium sized aquarium, and should be renewed every three months. The undergravel filter uses the whole aquarium bed as a filter and is left undisturbed to develop its full bacterial population. It acts as both a mechanical and biological filter and is never completely renewed at any one time. Frequently, depending on circumstances, it may be virtually undisturbed for years.

Available to the hobbyist are canister filters with quick-change cartridges. Easy to maintain, neat, and quick, these filters can be discussed with your local pet shop proprietor regarding their suitability for your miniature sea.

Carbon Filtration

High grade activated carbon removes over 50% of its own weight in toxins, gases, coloring matter and many other organic compounds from the water, but not many of the products of the nitrogen cycle. A simple box filter either inside or outside of the aquarium is all that's needed, containing the "sandwich" already described. One inside filter for medium tanks is the corner type, a ¼-circle box that fits into a back corner and can be hidden easily. Water flows in at the top via a perforated lid, through the sandwich, and is then raised up via a central airlift back to the tank. The airlift is a tube with a rising stream of bubbles that causes the whole gadget to work.

The composition and quality of your tank water is ever changing. To ensure the best possible environment for your sea life, kits that test the ammonia, nitrite, nitrate, pH, and copper levels are most helpful.

If you wish, a larger box filter may be hung at the top of the aquarium, either inside or outside. If inside, an airlift raises water over the top and into the filter. The water then gravitates through the sandwich and back into the tank. If outside, such a procedure would be dangerous, as the airlift could pump water out of the aquarium. So the flow is reversed, and the airlift pumps water back from the filter to the tank and syphons take it from the tank to the filter. The syphons and airlifts in these top filters are best provided with guards to prevent small critters from getting carried into the filters.

Undergravel Filtration

The nitrogen cycle in the aquarium is concerned with the breakdown of nitrogen-containing substances like proteins and their end-products, the principal of which is ammonia. Ammonia is very poisonous and also raises the pH, making the water more alkaline. In sea water, a given amount of ammonia is over ten times as toxic as in neutral water, as sea water has a pH of approximately 8.3. Ammonia is then toxic in less than 1 part per million or 1 mg/liter. In the undergravel filter, ammonia is converted first to nitrites, less toxic but still dangerous, and then to nitrates, which are harmless to fishes and many invertebrates unless present in large amounts (over 40 parts per million or mg/liter). This concentration of nitrates is taken care of by periodic water changes and sometimes by the growth of algae that use it as food.

There are two main types of undergravel filters. One consists of a network of perforated tubes buried in the gravel that "suck" the water through them by means of an airlift or two and return it to the surface. The other, often preferable in the marine aquarium, is a perforated plate or plates covering the entire base of the aquarium and raised about ½" (1 cm) above the glass bottom. Airlifts also perform the same function as in the first type or may be replaced in both cases by power-heads (small water pumps driven electrically). Coral sand, shell grit or any other suitable alkaline material is placed to a depth of about 3" on average over the plate. If it is coarse enough it will not fall through the plate, which should have slots of about ¹⁄₂₅" (1 mm), but we don't want it coarser than necessary, say ¹⁄₁₀" to ⅕" (2–4 mm) for safety. If you are in any doubt, some plastic flyscreen over the plate can solve the problem.

The filter works in aerobic conditions (in the presence of oxygen) so that, as the water passes through it, it will lose oxygen and gain carbon dioxide. By delivering it at the top of the tank, the water is reoxygenated. For the best effect, the water should be directed horizontally across the top. Some power-heads have an aerator built in to assist the process, but as this usually decreases the rate of flow, its use is questionable. The water should pass through the filter at about three times the tank volume per hour to give the best results. Reverse flow filters send the water the other way 'round—down under the plate and up through it into the aquarium.

Methods for starting up and conditioning undergravel filters are discussed in the next chapter. The point to be stressed is that they do not work immediately and that the bacterial growth is slow compared with most bacteria. Further, no matter how long you leave the filter running, without living creatures or a chemical treatment it will not develop the necessary bacterial population. This will grow satisfactorily only if you feed it with ammonia, either naturally or artificially. Hence, you cannot set up the aquarium and fill it with fishes, or anything else, straight away. If you do, you invite the "new tank

Designed to last a long time because they do not compact, the blue ball-like media allow bacteria to flourish, creating a highly effective biological filter.

syndrome" and your pets will succumb to ammonia poisoning, fall ill and probably die.

THE GRAVEL AND ROCKWORK

Besides providing a bed for bacterial growth, the gravel should help to maintain the mildly alkaline pH of sea water by being itself alkaline. Therefore we use coral sand, possibly shell grit or dolomite. Any rockwork may as well be alkaline too—old, compacted coral or of course coral skeletons themselves. Living coral can be kept only under very strict maintenance conditions with extra low nitrate levels and bright illumination (with some exceptions, such as those corals not containing indwelling algae).

AUXILIARY EQUIPMENT

We need to be able to measure the concentration of the salt water. For this, a *hydrometer* is required. The usual instrument floats in the water and has a long stem with graduations to be read just under the water surface, giving the specific gravity of the water. Pure water has a specific gravity of 1.000, typical sea water 1.025, at 60°F (15°C), for which the instrument is normally calibrated. At 80°F (27°C), the reading would

A power head can be attached to the top of an internal box filter to provide effective cleaning and circulation of the the tank water.

be 1.022 approximately, and allowance must be made for this. Some instruments for aquarists are now set for 75°F or 80°F (24°C or 27°C), so be careful! A new type of hydrometer can be obtained that has a pointer on a scale and sits under the water.

Don't forget a net, a syphon for cleaning the tank, a dip tube for removing uneaten food, etc., and a pair of long plastic tongs. You will also need a high quality salt mix, kits for measuring pH and nitrite concentration, and sodium bicarbonate for adjusting the pH. No other equipment is needed at this stage.

Water is the essential environment in which your fish live. The quality of the water therefore largely determines whether your fish thrive or just survive.

Not all fishes enjoy the same habitat. *Scorpaena cooki*, Cook's scorpionfish, for example, does best in a tank with coral heads on which it can perch, camouflaged, and do what it does best—ambush living prey.

Few people can visualize how an aquarium will look when they have finished setting it up, so it is worthwhile to make diagrams of what is intended, one from the front and one from the top. Do this so that you know where to put the heater, the filter and that large coral head that is a bit awkward to fit in. It makes a surprising difference to how fast you can

SETTING UP

work. Then proceed as follows:

1. Thoroughly wash everything in cold fresh water. Never use a household disinfectant except hydrogen peroxide or a chlorine bleach, and only if necessary, followed by several rinses in fresh water. Wash the coral sand or shell grit very thoroughly; it may need a dozen or more washings until the water runs off clear. Failure to do this can result in cloudy water that is difficult to get clean.

2. Fit the undergravel filter close against the back and sides of the aquarium but leave a small gap at the front so that it will not show. Connect up airlifts and then cover the filter with a double thickness of plastic flyscreen, tucking it down on all edges and fitting it snugly around the airlifts.

3. Cover the filter with several inches of wet gravel (dry gravel will float up when you add the water) and shape it so that it forms a shallow basin 3—4″ (7½—10 cm) at the back and not less than 2″ (5 cm) in the middle front. This aids an even flow of

Facing page: Setting up the tank requires consideration of the life forms that will soon inhabit the aquarium. The butterflyfishes, i.e. *Chaetodon semilarvatus* (two lower fish) and *Heniochus intermedius* (topmost fish), would well appreciate a large tank with few other of their species to avoid territorial disputes.

water, looks neat and encourages the collection of mulm at the front. Seed the gravel with the desired bacteria, preferably a commercial preparation, but in an emergency you can use a handful of gravel from an established *disease-free* tank or a few pinches of garden soil.

4. Place all equipment and corals, rocks, etc., in position. Fix leads and airlines in position by weighting them down with bits of rock or coral. See that the heater is not in any danger of becoming buried or touching the glass—do not trust suckers to do this. Make sure that *all* corals and rocks are safe to use. The coral should have been soaked in a bucket of fresh water if you are in any doubt; you will see or smell if it is not clean. Granite, marble, tufa, old compacted coral or iron-free sandstone are safe rocks.

5. Calculate the actual volume of the tank, subtract 20% as a rough estimate of the volume occupied by gravel, etc., and then dump in 4 oz. per gallon (28 g per liter) of high grade salt mix. If the mix has separate trace elements, keep these to add later. There is no need to dissolve the salts at this stage, as the water can be added in the aquarium. If your tap water contains only chlorine, it will blow off when you start the equipment, but if it has ammonia added, which forms chloramines with the chlorine, treat it after filling with water purifier.

6. Run a hose for 5–10 minutes until any static water in the pipes has cleared and then lead it into a bowl placed at center front of the aquarium. Turn on the water very gently so that it flows from the bowl onto the gravel with little disturbance. Do not allow any metallic hose connections to come into contact with the aquarium water, as the dissolving salt will attack them and poison the water. Half fill the tank and leave it for a few hours to let the salt dissolve and to guard against a leak—however unlikely. Then complete the filling. Some salt will still be un-

Above: If you opt to keep invertebrates in your tank, you must choose your fishes carefully.
Below: *Xanthichthys ringens,* the sargassum triggerfish, will gladly ingest your living rock.

The burgeoning marine community can bring living brilliance to any room of any home.

dissolved and the rest will be mainly a thick brine at the bottom, but not to worry.

7. Turn all equipment on and check that all is well. At first, the working of the undergravel filter may be erratic because of the partly dissolved salt, but it will soon clear itself and the salt will all dissolve, but may take several hours to do so. Next day, check the temperature; it should be between 76° and 80°F (24° and 27°C), and check the specific gravity. The latter should be between 1.022 and 1.023 to copy natural sea water, but if fishes are to be the only inhabitants, it can be as low as 1.018. Most fishes can acclimate to as low as 1.013, but then you have trouble when introducing new ones.

Setting Up

THE NEW TANK SYNDROME

Many an aquarium has been set up as carefully as above, and then the fishes have been put in and everything looked lovely for a week or so. Then, in the picturesque language of one author, "All hell breaks loose." Why? It took some time before we found out. The fishes were obviously unhappy, with drooping fins, scratching themselves on the surroundings and finally breaking out with obvious disease. We were lucky if any survived.

The answer lies in the workings of the nitrogen cycle. A tank that has not been carefully matured before introducing the fishes undergoes the establishment of the cycle in their presence. First a wave of ammonia accumulates because the bacteria (*Nitrosomas*) that will break it down into nitrites have yet to grow sufficiently to deal with it. Then a wave of nitrites accumulates for the reason that the next stage, conversion to nitrates, depends on the growth of further bacteria (*Nitrobacter*). Finally, after several weeks, all is well and only practically harmless nitrates build up. But by that time the harm is done. We must make sure that the cycle is working fully *before* introducing the fishes, or most of them.

Of direct relation to each other are the pH level and the toxicity of ammonia. In general, the higher the pH, the more toxic is ammonia. Ammonia is one of the prime killers of fish; correctly determining both the pH and ammonia level of the aquarium is vital to the success of your aquarium.

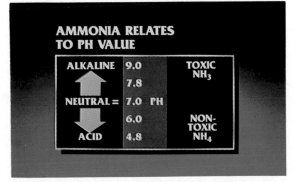

AMMONIA RELATES TO PH VALUE

ALKALINE	9.0	TOXIC NH$_3$
	7.8	
NEUTRAL =	7.0 PH	
	6.0	NON-TOXIC NH$_4$
ACID	4.8	

Above and below: Maturing the tank also involves maturing the biological filter, if employed. No tank, especially one that houses a miniature reef, is safe for the inclusion of marine life forms until both the tank and the filter are mature. Maturation largely involves the establishment of bacterial colonies sufficient to break ammonia into its less harmful components, nitrites and nitrates.

MATURING THE TANK

There are several ways to get the nitrogen cycle going safely. The oldest method is to put in a few tough fishes like clownfishes or *Dascyllus* and let them start things up, gradually introducing others over the next few weeks. Even just some rotting fish or meat could be used instead—anything to produce ammonia. So why not add ammonia itself? This leads us to the latest method that has theoretical advantages borne out in practice. First, most, if not all, fishes can be added together once the tank is safe. Second, by using as high an ammount of ammonia as feasible from the start, more of the bacteria in the gravel will be of the desired types, thus increasing the efficiency of the filter.

Both calculations and experience have evolved the following procedure: Make up a 10% solution of ammonium chloride or a 15% solution of ammonium sulphate (containing the same amount of ammonia). About ½ pint (250 ml) of solution will be needed per 25 gallons (100 liters) of aquarium water.

The degree of technology employed by the hobbyist depends on many variables. Some aquarists avidly affirm the use of complex electronic devices, while others strive to keep their hobby as "natural" as possible. Of course there are also many middle roads to travel. So long as the needs of the fishes are met, the complexity of your system is largely left to choice.

On days 1 and 2, add ½ teaspoon per 25 gallons (2½ ml per 100 liters); on days 3 and 4, add 1 teaspoon (5 ml) per 25 gallons and so on, increasing the dose by ½ teaspoon (2½ ml) per two days until 2 teaspoons (10 ml) per day is reached, and carry on at that level. Using a nitrite test kit, start measuring the nitrite level every other day from day 18 onward, when a peak should soon occur (up to 10 or 20 mg per liter). Stop treatment, wait a day or two and then put the fishes in—all of them if you wish.

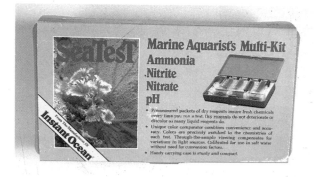

Test kits can help determine tank maturity.

If you read the literature you will find that others recommend smaller amounts of ammonia than here, but these only build the filter to less than its full capacity, and so waste time and effort and probably prevent the full capacity from ever being reached because other bacteria occupy the areas that would have been filled by the ones we want. A nitrite peak will still occur, but this is no guarantee that the filter is developing as full a capacity as it could.

FISH CAPACITY

The number of fishes that a given marine aquarium can hold is not as easy to define as with a freshwater aquarium. The general rule is to include fewer in the marine. Factors such as aeration, rate of feeding and rate of nitrification (conversion of ammonia) have a greater influence. To be on the safe side, particularly when starting up a tank, the following may be

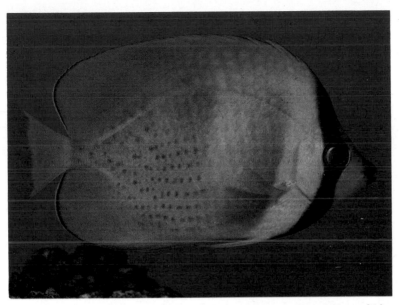

Chaetodon kleini, Klein's butterflyfish. Fish populations in the marine tank depend on such factors as tank volume, species housed, and filtration and aeration. Stocking the tank is not done by trial and error but by careful calculation and consideration.

taken as a guide. If you don't overfeed and do keep up good maintenance as indicated below, one 1″ to 2″ (2½–5 cm) fish can be accomodated per 5 gallons (20 liters). This allows for growth to 2″ to 4″ (5–10 cm). As the tank matures, the allowance of water can probably be lowered to 3 gallons (12 liters) per fish, but not all can be as large as 4″. With tender fishes, such as most chaetodons, more room should be allowed.

This means that a 25 gallon (100 liter) tank should have five fishes, and a 50 gallon (200 liter) tank about ten fishes to start with and a few more later on. With nutritious but careful feeding, the fishes will flourish but not grow too quickly. Watch their growth and, unless you want them to grow rapidly, cut down on the food a bit if they do. Fishes are very good at making the best of their food and do not suffer from undernourishment in the way that a mammal does; simply they don't grow much. They can even breed at a fraction of the normal weight for the species.

MAINTENANCE

An aquarium needs regular attention. Depending on exactly how it is set up, the attention required will vary, but for one set up as suggested, the following would be sensible rules.

Daily: Check the temperature and general appearance, look for each fish or large invertebrate to see that all is well. Feed sparingly morning and evening and see that each fish eats. Never feed more than is consumed almost immediately, and remove any uneaten food.

Weekly: Clean the front glass but not the back and sides unless you want to. Clean the top covers if necessary. Check the pH for the first few weeks and correct it if necessary. Whatever the pH, add 1 teaspoon (5 ml) per 25 gallons (100 liters) of sodium bicarbonate to keep the buffer capacity of the salt water (this is its reserve of alkali on which stability of pH depends). Add more than 1 teaspoon if the pH needs raising, i.e., if it is below 8.0.

Monthly: Syphon off 20–25% of the water and replace it with new water that has been aerated or treated for chloramines and is at the correct temperature. When syphoning, lift rocks and coral where feasible and disturb the top of the gravel to remove debris

Left: Many supplies are found at your local pet shop. These tools can help keep the tank clean and vibrant and your hobby productively growing. **Facing page:** Regular maintenance helps ensure success.

and mulm. Check the pH, nitrite level and specific gravity after replacing the water. It may be necessary to add a little fresh water to make up for evaporation. See if the top pad of the carbon filter needs replacing; this may be needed more often than monthly.

Quarterly: Renew the carbon filter completely, washing the new carbon before use. If the rocks and coral are getting covered by too much algae, remove some of it, but not all. It looks nice to have a mixture of clean and algae-covered decorations and it is a good idea to have a few spares and circulate them through the tank. Coral is best bleached in the sun, but a household bleach followed by a very thorough washing is O.K.

Yearly: Syphon off about one-third of the gravel. If a lot of sediment swirls up when you disturb it, wash it and replace it. Never remove most of the gravel at one time or you will lose too many of the beneficial bacteria. After such a clean-up, feed very lightly for the next week, as you have weakened the capacity of the undergravel filter to deal with ammonia. Check over all equipment carefully and renew any suspicious diaphragms, gang-valves, tubing, airstones, etc. Airstones may need more frequent cleaning or replacement.

FISHES

The fishes you will be keeping will come mostly or entirely from coral reefs. They will be accustomed to "owning" a piece of the reef—quite often just a few square feet—and this makes them inclined to be aggressive. Their aggression is usually quite selective and not aimed at other species that are not rivals for food or shelter. So two angelfishes of different species may not get on at all, while tolerating some damsels or anemonefishes. It pays to read up about any fish you want to buy and to decide whether it will be likely to fit in with the others, or at least to discuss the question with your dealer or friends.

Compatibility is not the only thing to worry about. Consider how large any particular fish can grow, how easy it is to feed and what sort of reputation it has for surviving in the aquarium. There are plenty of fishes from which to choose, so don't handicap yourself by choosing difficult ones to start with. Don't think that because you see groups of fishes apparently happy together in a pet shop they will stay that way in your aquarium. They are probably crowded and new to their surroundings and haven't yet had the chance to become territorial. Give them room in a nice quiet environment and they will behave quite differently. Also, don't normally buy "pairs" as is the custom with freshwater fishes; they are the most likely to hate each other unless they are a true pair.

Some fishes are notoriously difficult for one reason or another. Many triggers are too mean to mix with most fishes, the clown trigger *(Balistoides conspicillum)* in particular. So are most groupers that look most attractive when young but grow

Facing page: *Acanthurus achilles*, the Achilles tang, is one of the many attractive fishes commonly kept in the hobby.

up into predatory horrors. Others just won't eat or are too finicky and slow to be kept with any but other fishes of their own persuasion. Sea horses (*Hippocampus* species) and mandarins (*Synchiropus* species) are such slow eaters that they must be kept separate from normal fishes. Some of the chaetodons (butterflyfishes) are such specialist feeders, on coral, for example, that it is virtually impossible to feed them adequately. Yet you get the exception that decides to eat tubifex, or something else that it would never encounter naturally, and flourishes!

BUYING A FISH

Years ago, I spent a lot of time visiting pet shops and buying a fish here and another there, until I started to keep records, particularly of my purchases of marines. Then I made a discovery—that the fishes from only one or two sources thrived and lived much longer in my tanks than from all the others. There was no obligatory quarantine of marine fishes and so I made inquiries as diplomatically as possible about the sources and subsequent treatment of fishes in different shops. What emerged fairly clearly was that the fishes that did well came from establishments that imposed their own voluntary quarantine, plus treatment of any diseases that became apparent. Probably just holding the fishes for a week or so helped considerably, giving them a much needed rest instead of a rapid transfer to yet another tank. Whether I imposed a further quarantine period or not, they did better.

It pays to get to know your supplier and his habits and to reward the conscientious ones with your trade. Then, wherever you are, look carefully around you before making a purchase and assess the housekeeping. Buy nothing from a tank that has even one sick fish in it. Torn fins or tail, if not inflamed or badly torn, mean little, as marines tend to fight, but accept nothing worse. Buy only alert, plump fishes, and if in doubt, ask the dealer to feed your intended purchase. Today we have the problem of cyanide-caught fishes that can look good yet will die in a few weeks because they have been poisoned. You cannot tell this from even careful examination by eye, so you must ask pointblank whether you can be assured that a fish has not been caught with cyanide.

Ecsenius lineatus, Klausewitz's blenny, is one very colorful blenny native to the Indian Ocean. Blennies are typically small, non-aggressive creatures and prey for many larger ones. They should be kept with compatibly small, peaceful fishes and provided with sufficient hiding places.

Other signs to look for before purchase are rapid breathing and general behavior. Small fishes in health respire at 80–100 per minute, larger ones even slower, and anything more rapid signals distress and possible infection. So, of course, does glancing off rocks and corals, clamped fins or permanently erect fins, cloudy eyes and any sign of damage around the mouth. A fish should not be hiding away, unless he is a wrasse or a goby, many of which do so normally. The majority, however, swim around freely if in health and not recently disturbed.

Finally, watch how the fish is caught out of the tank and walk out of the premises if it is subjected to a long chase and potential damage. Ideally, it should be gently steered into a plastic bag under the water. This may be asking too much, but it must not be stressed or damaged by inexpert handling as too often is the case. A wise dealer doesn't clutter up his tanks with decorations except for the needs of his fishes and uses two reasonably large nets to catch out a fish. This is then transferred carefully to a plastic bag, only one fish per bag, which is oxygenated unless the journey home is very short.

TRANSPORT AND TRANSFER

The bags containing the purchases should be carried in an insulated box to keep them at the same temperature as far as possible. You must expect to supply this yourself. When you get them home, don't suddenly open the box and shock the fishes with a flood of light. Do it gradually so that they remain calm and ready for transfer to the tank. This may be a quarantine tank or the display tank, depending on circumstances and how careful you are.

Check the temperature and pH of the tank and of the water of transport, and if either differs by more than a few degrees (say 3°F or 2°C) or 0.5 in pH, take an hour or two hours over the transfer; if not, half an hour will suffice. Float each bag in the tank and gradually replace the water with water from the tank, using a baster or large syringe. Change ¼ to ⅓ of the

Coris aygula, the clown coris. Members of the genus *Coris* typically grow to a large size, suitable for only the large aquarium.

water in the bag every 10–30 minutes, according to the magnitude of the difference in pH or temperature. If there is a difference in salinity, the technique takes care of this as well. Watch the behavior of any fishes already in the tank towards the newcomers, and if there is any sign of aggression, be wary about the next move.

When ready, gently tip the bag so that the fish can swim free, and watch for any trouble. Some fishes swim around and nibble the algae as though they owned the place, others dash for safety, and some tangs frighten the life out of their new owner by lying on the bottom as though about to die but recover later. If there is severe bickering, turn off the lights; this will often stop it. If it continues, shift the scenery around if feasible, as this often confuses the inhabitants and stops trouble. As a last resort, you may have to remove either the victim or the bully and try again after floating him in an aerated jug or bag for a period.

QUARANTINE AND OTHER MEASURES

Let's face it—many of us are not going to maintain a separate quarantine tank and so must be all the more careful along the lines suggested above. Most often we'll get away with it, but sooner or later we're going to be sorry! Fishes often have a degree of immunity to some of the more common diseases and so, with otherwise good management, we get away with taking risks. Then comes a specimen with a new strain or a new disease and we are in trouble. A perfectly healthy new fish can even catch something from your tank that is never actually sterile, and quarantine isn't going to stop that.

Quarantine practices vary. Many aquarists keep new fishes in a reserve tank without treatment for several weeks, and if nothing develops, they transfer them to an exhibition tank. Others add a treatment of some kind to this procedure, usually copper or copper plus formalin. Some precede this with immersion in fresh water for a minute or two, watching to see that the fish is not too seriously stressed and removing it if it is. The freshwater dunk bursts the cysts of surface parasites and helps to ensure safety. Some use just the freshwater dunk and a brief immersion in strong copper-formalin and then put the fish straight into the main aquarium. My own choice is quarantine with copper alone, which, when properly done, gets rid of velvet and white spot, the two chief diseases that plague new marine fishes.

If you are not going to quarantine newcomers, you can treat the whole tank each time you introduce them, as long as it isn't done too often and as long as you keep only fishes. After conditioning the aquarium chemically with ammonium salts, the first main batch of fishes can be treated in the tank. A few new fishes may be added over the next few weeks and the copper treatment kept up until two weeks after the last introduction, monitoring the copper level with a kit.

After treating a tank with copper, it is not safe to put invertebrates in for weeks or months, depending on what you use and the exact conditions in the tank. If copper sulphate or citrate is used and then cleared up with carbon or a resin and checked with a copper kit, most invertebrates can be introduced after a few weeks, but if a complex copper preparation

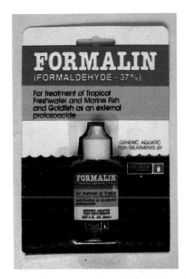

Among chemical treatments for external parasites are copper and formalin. In the correct doses these and other chemical preparations can prove most helpful to the aquarist. However, many substances can prove damaging to the fishes on which they are used if not used as directed.

has been employed, it is usual to recommend at least four months before the aquarium will be safe for invertebrates. Moreover, a copper kit cannot measure the level of copper accurately after such a preparation has been used, and so we have no guide to what is happening.

However, don't despair! A mixed tank of fishes and invertebrates, set up as recommended, and preferably with plenty of filter feeders and/or living rock, is a very healthy environment and disease resistant to a good degree. You won't keep too many fishes if much invertebrate life is present. This fact, plus the disease-preventing properties of filter feeders, which mop up a lot of the free-swimming stages of diseases like white spot, helps keep the peril down. There is no guarantee, of course, but experience shows that even untreated mild outbreaks tend to disappear without serious trouble, leaving the fishes with a degree of immunity.

The foregoing reference to living rock is to old, usually compacted coral that has been colonized by various inverte-

brates such as tube worms, small crustaceans, soft corals, sponges, and various other critters, plus algae. Obtained fresh for preference, or properly cured by your dealer, when it takes longer to develop, it acts as an additional nitrifier and adds to the health of the tank as long as it is adequately lit. Such a set-up is usually referred to as a semi-natural system, the use of an undergravel filter and carbon filter distinguishing it from the purely natural system that uses living rock and invertebrates without filters.

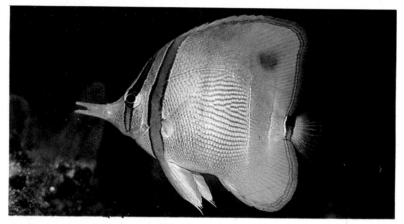

Feeding on invertebrates and enjoying good lighting, *Chelmon marginalis*, commonly known as Willemawillum, is not commonly kept in the hobby.

FISHES TO KEEP

The following fishes are relatively easy to keep and not too expensive: damselfishes, including anemonefishes with or without anemones; *Chromis* species; *Dascyllus* species, except *D. trimaculatus* (3-spot *Dascyllus*) that gets too big and pugnacious; *Abudefduf* (Sergeant majors); many wrasses, gobies and blennies; cardinalfishes; some puffers; most of the pygmy angels (*Centropyge* species); and *Heniochus* species.

The next group of fishes is somewhat more difficult, usually more expensive as well: chaetodons; *Chelmon rostratus*; surgeons and tangs; filefishes; sea perches; the larger marine angels, many of which get too large as well as being difficult.

Balistoides conspicillum, the clown triggerfish, is a feisty fish that can grow rather large and pugnacious. It is best suited for an "indestructible" aquarium of its own.

FISHES TO AVOID

Groupers, most triggerfishes, lionfishes, and angler-fishes must be kept only with other large fishes, as all are predatory or very pugnacious. Small groupers often look very attractive, but beware! Batfishes also grow prodigiously and lose their attractiveness at the same time. Some chaetodons are almost impossible to keep or feed, so look up any you propose to purchase before doing so. *Pygoplites diacanthus* (the regal angelfish) nearly always starves away; so does *Zanclus canescens* (the Moorish idol) in any but expert hands.

Below: This vibrant pseudo-psychedelic school of *Acanthurus leucosternon* (powder-blue tangs) reveals behavior in the wild not commonly observable in the captive state. Many species of marine fish swarm in large groups about the natural reef. In the aquarium, however, the space available is so necessarily limited that introducing too many of the same species results in territorial disputes and not attractive schools. Depending on the severity, territorial disputes can lead to lethal combat. **Facing page:** *Centropyge flavissimus*, commonly known as lemonpeel, is a hardy fish of brilliant yellow.

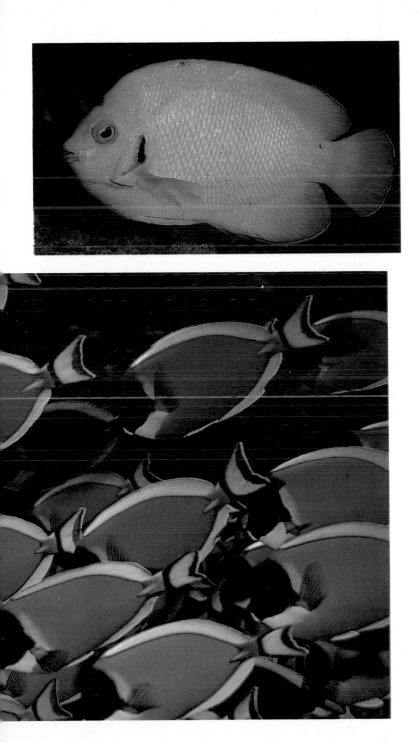

OTHER MARINES

Although this is quite a small book on marine aquaria and the majority of books for beginners do not include invertebrates, this one will do so. This is because half or more than half of the pleasure of keeping a salt water tank is lost if invertebrates are not cultivated. The proportion of fishes to invertebrates is up to you; it may only be an anemone and shrimp or two with the fishes or, at the other extreme, just a few fishes in a predominantly invertebrate aquarium. To mix the two is always more difficult than keeping only fishes or only invertebrates, but not vastly more difficult. However, if you are a complete beginner, it would be advisable to start off with fishes on their own to gain some general experience before adding the invertebrates. You could start the other way around, but except for natural system enthusiasts, nobody seems to do so.

The main difficulty in keeping fishes with invertebrates is the treatment of fish diseases and parasites, as some of the popular cures are fatal to most invertebrates. Copper is lethal to crustaceans and many others and it also kills algae, desirable in a mixed tank. Most other medicines affect one species or another, so it is best at first to keep invertebrates that can readily be removed from the tank while any cure is being attempted.

Invertebrates fall into many different phyla—groups of animals built on the same basic plan. Fishes all belong to a single subdivision (Class Pisces) of a single phylum, the Chordata, possessors of a notochord.

Facing page: It is generally believed that invertebrates are not for beginners. However, any person dedicated enough to approach the keeping of these marine life forms with knowledge and consideration can likely experience success.

PHYLUM CNIDARIA

This includes the anemones and corals plus a host of similarly built creatures. They have radial symmetry, like the spokes of a wheel, a single opening into a central cavity and produce nematocysts, stinging cells that send out poisonous darts when touched. Anemones are much easier to keep than living corals, although some of the popular anemones share with many corals the possession of indwelling algae (*Zoochlorellae* and *Zooxanthellae*) and must be very well illuminated to flourish.

For some, anemones and other invertebrates are most fascinating creatures without which their hobby would be incomplete.

Other Marines

You are likely to be attracted to the keeping of anemonefishes with one or more of the large tropical anemones they frequent, and this is a very nice introduction to invertebrates. These stichodactyline anemones have indwelling algae and feed both on the algal products and on prey caught by their tentacles or on food brought to them by the anemonefishes. Popular species fall into the genera *Radianthus*, with long tentacles, or *Stoichactis* and *Discosoma*, with mostly small tentacles, looking like a piece of towelling. Different species of anemonefish vary in the extent to which they "feed" their anemones or use them as a storage-place. The common anemonefish *Amphiphrion ocellaris* is more inclined to steal food from its host than to feed it.

There are many species of small anemones that are kept for their own beauty, and some will reproduce in the aquarium by splitting into two, by budding off young or by sexual reproduction that in some results in incubating the young in the central cavity and eventually ejecting them to the surroundings. Not all anemones are welcome in the aquarium. The genus *Cerianthus* of tube-building anemones has some very attractive members, pastel-colored with long trailing tentacles, but they are lethal and will kill small creatures, even including crustaceans that can normally escape an anemone unhurt. Even worse is the fire anemone, *Actinodendron* sp., looking like a small tree with many branching arms, that can inflict nasty stings on its owner as well as its tank-mates.

The corals fall into three types. Soft corals have spicules of lime in their tissues but do not form hard skeletons. As they do not usually contain algae, they get along well in subdued lighting, but they mostly demand purer water, low in nitrates as well as other pollutants, than do anemones. Solitary corals do not build reefs although they construct hard limey skeletons. A favorite is the genus *Fungia*, the mushroom corals, each of which consists of a single large polyp sitting on the substrate and is variously colored. Reef-builders are on the whole harder to keep, demanding pure water, bright light, and water movement to stay alive in the aquarium. Moreover, only some species open in the daytime to be enjoyed by the aquarist. Perhaps the best to try when you feel equal to it are *Goniopora*

species, characteristically with long polyps of varied colors, many of which do open in the daylight. They feed both from their algae and from plankton and so should be fed occasionally and kept well illuminated. As with many corals, the *Goniopora* are not good neighbors to other corals or anemones; they will stretch out their polyps to a surprising length to sting them. Yet they tolerate anemonefishes that find them acceptable as hosts in the aquarium.

PHYLUM ARTHROPODA

This enormous group of animals includes all those with hard, external skeletons and jointed limbs, including the insects, spiders, crustaceans and ticks. Only the crustaceans inhabit the sea as well as fresh waters and even dry land, and there are very many species. Easy to keep, shrimps and crabs are popular aquarium species, but large crabs and, in fact, most large crustaceans are best avoided; they are too destructive. Attractive as some of the tropical lobsters are when tiny, don't forget that they can grow rapidly into beautiful but annoying pests that upset the scenery, grope into anemones for food, and even catch your favorite fish. Hermit crabs are tolerable when small, but any that grow large will eventually prove difficult. If you wish to try them, don't forget their need for bigger and bigger shells as they grow up.

There are some very nice shrimps that won't grow large and can be enjoyed as long as they live. The frequently kept banded coral shrimp, *Stenopus hispidus*, is tough and entertaining. Try to obtain a mated pair. Individuals of the same sex fight, but a pair is delightful. They go around together frequently, look after each other when one is molting, and the male feeds the female even at his own expense. They are hostile to other shrimps, but not dangerously so, merely chasing them away. They stalk around the aquarium rather like scorpions, with two large claws extended, and grow to about 3" (7½ cm) in length at most. As with all crustaceans, they shed the integument at intervals and regrow lost claws or legs. They are also rather ineffective cleaners, picking parasites off fishes if they feel like it, but they aren't very keen on the job, in my own experience.

Attractive though rather seclusive is the porcelain crab *Petrolisthes galathinus*, an Atlantic species of non-aggressive, filter-feeding invertebrates.

Another equally attractive shrimp is *Lysmata grabhami*, a cleaner with red stripes that is not aggressive and can be kept in groups. Various shrimps, like the genus *Periclimenes*, live on the tropical anemones and feed on scraps from their table. Shrimps to be avoided are any of the mantis shrimps, *Squilla* and others that are predatory and have very sharp appendages that can damage other inhabitants and slash the hand that feeds them. The harlequin shrimps, genus *Hymenocerus*, are very attractive but feed on the tube feet of starfishes. If you don't keep starfishes, these shrimps may allegedly be adapted to other foods with some difficulty.

There are about as many species of crabs available as there are shrimps. Some of the decorator crabs of various genera are amusing to keep, covering themselves with bits of the scenery or with small anemones that they carefully transfer to their new carapace after a molt. Many crabs, however, are so shy that they are not worth having, hiding away all day and emerging only at night. If you add some living rock to your aquarium, you may be surprised at how many crabs you eventually possess as they grow up and become apparent. Desirable crabs include some of the anemone crabs, like *Porcellana*, and the arrow crab, *Stenorhyncus seticornis*, with its long legs and orange or red stripes. If you have a selection of crabs, you may be surprised one day by a swarm of *nauplii*, newly hatched young like those of the the brine shrimp. They won't last long as they provide a welcome snack to the tank's inhabitants.

PHYLUM ECHINODERMATA

This phylum has five classes, all of interest to the aquarist: the Crinoidea, sea lilies and feather stars; the Holothuroidea, sea cucumbers; the Echinoidea, sea urchins; the Asteroidea, sea stars; and the Ophiuroidea, brittle stars.

The sea lilies flourished millions of years ago and are now almost confined to deep waters. They are like feather stars on stalks, and the feather stars themselves are stalked when young and then break free. Like all other echinoderms, they have radial symmetry and a water vascular system that furnishes hydraulic power to the tube feet, characteristic of the phylum and used both for locomotion and catching prey. Although attractive, crinoids are very liable to break up or be broken up in the aquarium by fishes, crabs, etc. They are filter feeders and otherwise fairly easy to keep.

Sea cucumbers are mostly uninteresting slug-like creatures that crawl around the bottom ingesting debris, but the family Dendrochirotidae, sea apples, etc., is brilliantly colored

Members of the genus *Fromia*, such as this Indo-Pacific starfish, are attractive but often prefer temperate waters.

In the lower portion of this photo is one of the many feather duster worms that are commonly kept in the hobby.

and plankton feeding. Various members are bright red or red, white, and blue with a ring of large showy tentacles around the mouth. The latter may be shed and slowly grown again.

Sea urchins are spherical or nearly so in shape and calcified, so that when dead they leave a hard skeleton. They are mostly scavengers and algae eaters or omnivores, doing well in the aquarium as long as food is present. Some have long spines by which they move around, as well as by their tube feet. Others have very short spines, yet others venomous ones, so be careful. The slate-pencil urchin, *Heterocentrotus*, has thick spines adapted to rough surf but does well in the aquarium.

The sea stars or starfishes are the echinoderms most often kept, but not all do well in the aquarium and some are extremely predatory. A typical five-armed or multi-armed starfish preys predominantly on bivalve mollusks in nature and of course in the aquarium if they are available. It attaches its tube feet to the two halves of the shell and exerts a steady pull until the mollusk weakens and opens up a little. Then the starfish inserts its stomach into the shell and starts digestion. Other stars are debris feeders or omnivores and can be very destructive in the aquarium. An interesting case is the commonly kept blue star, *Linckia laevigata*, that in the experience of most people lives on for months or years without seeming to eat at all, yet at least one aquarist found one suddenly devastated his living rock.

Brittle stars are rather difficult on the whole, readily breaking up and also hiding away most of the time, although they learn to emerge when suitable food is presented. However, some of the larger species such as *Ophiarachnella* are rubbery and do not break up easily and scuttle around like spiders, seizing prey by coiling an arm or arms around it.

PHYLUM ANNELIDA

This is the group of segmented worms that includes the earthworms, tubificids, feather duster worms and many other tube worms. Only the polychaete worms, and of those, the tube builders, are of aquarium interest. Your tank may be the host to thousands of other worms of different phyla, but you will be mostly interested in them as scavengers or food for other inhabitants. The serpulid worms build calcareous tubes from which the head emerges with a circle or circles of tentacles branching out to feed on plankton. They come in all sizes, from quite tiny ones to those with a crown of tentacles 4″ or 5″ (10 or 12½ cm) across. Most, of whatever size, have some colorful varieties and can present a display of red, white, blue, brown, and speckled all in one colony. The sabellids construct leathery tubes and offer many colorful species. The serpulid *Spirobranchius* has corkscrew crowns up to 2″ (5 cm) across and of many different colors. All of these worms may be called fan or feather duster worms and are easily fed on fine food suspensions or newly hatched brine shrimp. They retire into their tubes so rapidly on being disturbed that they mostly escape predation, but devoted predators such as mandarin fishes can get them in the end.

PHYLUM MOLLUSCA

Second only in number of species to the Arthropoda, the mollusks are soft-bodied animals that usually secrete a shell, are bilaterally symmetrical and have a muscular foot and usually a rasping organ or tongue, the radula.

Univalve mollusks have a head, usually bearing eyes, typified by the common snails. They are often present in the aquarium by accident; tiny limpets and winkle- and whelk-like forms grow up from larvae and eventually manifest themselves. Purposely kept specimens of cowries, genus *Cypraea*, are popular, as the body extends in part as a decorative mantle over the outside of an often decorative shell when the animal is active. However, the food of cowries has been poorly researched and we are not clear what some of them devour. Other univalves may be dangerous, such as the cone shells that bear poisonous tips to the radulas and whelks in general that feed on other mollusks.

Sea hares and nudibranchs (pronounced nu-dee-brank) have no visible shell, although one may be buried under the skin. The sea hares, *Tethys* and other genera, are vegetarians and can do well in the aquarium, but nudibranchs are carnivorous and often feed on very special prey such as corals, sponges and hydroid polyps and are difficult to keep. This is a great pity as they are often very colorful and attractive, with waving external gills and an active life-style.

Bivalve mollusks have a hinged shell and include clams, mussels, oysters, and scallops; all are filter feeders needing a good supply of plankton or a suitable substitute. Many clams have indwelling algae and can get along if well illuminated, but most bivalves do not. Scallops are popular as they are active and can move around by jets of water expelled from the hinges of the shell or by flapping the shell. *Lima*, a frequently kept genus, is red or pink in color with a fringe of long tentacles.

Cephalopods (head-footed mollusks) include the squids and octopuses that are often highly intelligent for invertebrates and endowed with good memories. They are not, however, for the normal aquarium, as they are predatory, liable to foul the water with their ink if worried, and many can inflict a poison-

Cypraea cervus, the Atlantic deer cowry, is one of the many algae-feeding cowries found around the world. Most are subtropical to tropical and are especially suited to aquariums in need of algae control.

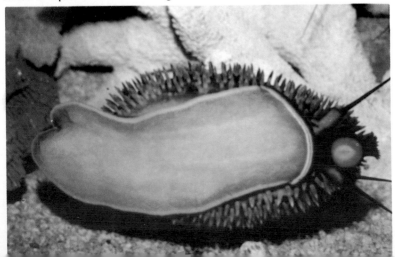

ous bite. Octopuses in particular are also accomplished escapers and can squeeze through an incredibly small gap.

ALGAE

Encrusting and possibly hair-like algae will grow unasked in a well-lit aquarium. They help to purify the water and are food for many of the inhabitants. Although they may need to be cleaned off the glass and rocks or corals, never remove them completely. Higher algae, characterized by a plant body, or *thallus*, need usually to be introduced. Most of those of value in the aquarium are green algae, but there are some attractive red or brown ones as well. All possess the green pigment chlorophyll; the reds and browns have other pigments in addition that mask it. These algae have complex life histories with alternation of generations so that the "offspring" of one generation is often quite different in appearance from its parent and you will not recognize it if it grows up in the aquarium.

Among the green algae, various species of *Caulerpa* are popular because they will reproduce from fragments or cuttings, whereas few others do this. *Caulerpa* come in species with flat green fronds (*C. prolifera*), fern-like fronds (*C. mexicana, C. lanuginosa* and others), rounded knobs like bunches of grapes (*C. racemosa* and *C. peltata*), even like cacti (*C. cupressoides*). Other useful green algae are calcareous, with limey thalluses, and must be obtained with a holdfast stuck onto a rock or other firm base. They do not reproduce from fragments. *Halimeda* species resemble cacti, with jointed segments. *H. discoidea* (baby bows) has circular segments up to 1″ (2½ cm) across. The sea fans *(Udotea* species) have a flattened thallus, while Neptune's shaving brush *(Pencillus capitatus)* looks as indicated. The sea lettuces *(Ulva* or *Monostroma)* are so attractive as food that they rarely survive for long.

Red algae mostly flourish in poorer light than the greens and are for the most part small and tough and worth cultivating. There are red hair-like algae and encrusting forms, but the really attractive types include *Pterocladia* species, branching red or russet plants 3″—4″ (7½—10 cm) in size, *Laurencia* species, branching and fern-like, and the limey genera *Corallina, Jania* and *Amphiroa,* common on living rock and drying out as white skeletons.

The growth of algae is to be encouraged, especially of the higher forms, such as the caulperpa at the top of the photo. At the bottom of the photo is seen the common filamentous type algae that often demands considerable cultivation to prevent its taking over your tank.

Brown algae need to be treated with care, as they tend to be slimy, release toxins and foul the tank. Those that occur spontaneously on living rock are safe. They come in calcified and non-calcified species just like the others, often hard to identify. The genus *Padina* produces small brown fans, lightly calcified, while *Dictyota* and *Dilophus* grow like brown editions of sea lettuce.

53

Luckily for the aquarist many species of fish will accept foods that are quite foreign to them; those that are hard to keep are often the ones that will not depart from their native diets. If a fish normally eats coral polyps, it is difficult to feed if it won't accept anything else! Sometimes you can trick it into eating tubificids stuffed into a coral skeleton; sometimes you can't. It is very useful, therefore, to know what a fish eats normally, in case difficulties arise in getting it to feed in the aquarium, also in order to give it an approximation to its natural food. In brief presentation, it seems easiest to group the fishes into broad classes for discussion.

FEEDING

CARNIVORES

Predatory fishes that eat small fishes, crabs, shrimps, gastropods and even sea urchins are easy to feed, as they usually learn to take some chunks of dead material or frozen lancefish and the like. These include lionfishes, groupers, triggers and wrasses.

Plankton feeders, eating primarily zooplankton, are easy to feed on live, frozen or dried preparations such as brine shrimp, small marine plankton itself and even crushed flakes or pellets. Many damselfishes eat mostly zooplankton, so do young angels and chaetodons and the young of many other species, some of which go through a phase of cleaning other fishes.

Feeders on cnidarians (anemones, corals etc.), sponges, tunicates and other benthic animals are often difficult; but, if caught young and fed at first on substitutes for zooplank-

ton, some will allow themselves to be weaned onto other foods, even flakes and other dried foods. This is true of many angelfishes and chaetodons. Chaetodons that will not usually make the change and are thus notoriously hard to keep include *Chaetodon trifasciatus, C. meyeri, C. ornatissimus* and *C. triangulum.* Angelfishes mostly feed on sponges, corals, anemones and other difficult foods, but most of them will change over to other foods, particularly if raised from juvenile stages in the aquarium. *Pygoplites diacanthus*, the regal angel, won't easily accept such a change and often starves as a result.

OMNIVORES

Many carnivores eat a little algae, but by omnivores is meant those fishes that normally choose a mixed diet. These are easy to cater to in the aquarium and often accept almost any food of the right size.

The easy-to-keep chaetodons, such as *C. ephippium* and *C. vagabundus*, are omnivores, so are many damselfishes such as *Abudefduf* species and the *Amphiprions.*

HERBIVORES

Notorious herbivores are the surgeonfishes, or tangs, but the parrotfishes, pomacentrid damsels and Moorish idols are also herbivores. Anyone who places a tang into a natural system or mini-reef tank can testify to its herbivorous nature! Most herbivores will eat some animal food as well, but do not thrive if they do not get plenty of greens. If there is not sufficient algae in the aquarium, substitutes must be provided in the form of previously frozen lettuce, spinach or other green vegetables. Why previously frozen? Because the fishes will accept the mushy thawed vegetation more readily than the fresh, crisp article. Perhaps it resembles seaweeds.

LIVE FOODS

It is best not to feed anything direct from the sea or the fishmonger because of the danger of disease or parasites. It is much safer to feed marine fishes on creatures from fresh water sources. They will live long enough to be eaten, and some, such as insect larvae, will live for hours in salt water. An excep-

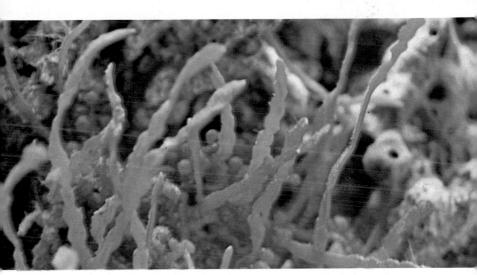

Omnivorous and herbivorous fishes require plant matter such as algae, shown above. A tank full of algae-eating fishes will likely prevent your achieving an algae bed sufficient for your fishes' dietary needs—in which case algae may have to be cultivated in a separate tank or purchased at a local pet shop.

tion is the brine shrimp, coming as dried "eggs," themselves from strong brine or as adults on sale in the pet shop. There may be some danger from the latter, depending on exactly what they are swimming in, so enquire if feasible.

Brine Shrimp (*Artemia salina*)

This is an excellent food, fed as newly hatched young (*nauplii*) to juvenile and small fishes or as part or fully grown shrimps to bigger fishes. The dried "eggs" are really arrested early stages of development that continue when they are placed in salt water. Half- to full-strength sea water will do, preferably at about 80°F (27°C), not below 70°F (21°C) or they will not hatch. The eggs will hatch if floated carefully on the surface of shallow trays of water at not more than ½-teaspoon per gallon (4 liters), and the *nauplii* can be collected one or two days later. They are attracted to light and can be syphoned off, leaving the floating shells behind. For large batches, the eggs may be aerated briskly in ¾-full gallon jars at 1 teaspoon per gallon. When the air is turned off, some eggshells will float, some will sink, and the *nauplii* can be syphoned off as before. Special hatching kits may also be bought if you prefer to do so.

Live foods such as brine shrimp are readily available at your local pet shop. Brine shrimp can be fed at their various stages of development, depending on the size of the fish that is to consume them.

Adult shrimps may be grown in a brine consisting of 10 oz. (280 g) of common salt, 2 oz. (56 g) of Epsom salts and 1 oz. (28 g) of bicarbonate of soda per gallon (4 liters). (This is for San Francisco eggs; those from other sources may need a different brine.) Place about 500 nauplii per gallon and feed on baker's yeast, just a pinch renewed as the brine clears. If you plan to feed half-grown shrimps, use more per gallon. They will attain full size in six to eight weeks.

Brine shrimp eggs may be bought already shelled, which gives a better hatch, or they may be placed straight into the marine aquarium to be eaten or to hatch and then be eaten. They float around and then settle on the bottom if not consumed.

Worms

Microworms, grindal worms and white worms are all suitable for marines if not fed too often, as they are full of saturated fats. They can be cultivated at home or bought from your pet shop. Microworms are quite tiny and can be fed to fry; the others are eaten by fishes of up to 2" (5 cm) in length, but are usually ignored by larger ones.

Tubificid worms (tubifex), well cleaned by storage under a dripping tap, are readily taken by some fussy eaters and are of value in getting them to feed, but again should not be fed to excess. Earthworms, whole for big fishes and chopped up for smaller ones, are another favorite treat.

Insect Larvae

Mosquito larvae are an excellent food and will survive in the marine tank without consuming oxygen. Collect them from fish-free ponds, as some diseases are common to fresh- and saltwater fishes. Sort into sizes, if necessary, with kitchen sieves and store in fresh water in sealed jars in the refrigerator—but not for too long or they may pupate and hatch. The larger bloodworm (*Chironomus*) and glassworm (*Chaoborus*) are gnat larvae that may occasionally be collected and fed to the bigger fishes.

Water Fleas

Daphnia pulex, the water flea, can be collected from ponds also, and is sometimes on sale. It swarms as reddish or greenish masses in mid-water, depending on its diet and the

Supplementing the sea-animal's food consumption with a variety of food forms is one way of increasing the likelihood of nutritional soundness.

strain of fleas, and can be stored as for mosquito larvae. It can be cultivated successfully only in large vats of 50 gallons (200 liters) or more, if fed on liver powder, dried blood or other rich foods and kept fairly cool, say under 70°F (21°C) if possible. Other small crustaceans may be encountered from time to time and are quite suitable as fish food in the marine tank.

Preserved Foods

Foods may be preserved by drying, by freezing or by both together, producing freeze-dried products. Frozen foods are the next best to live foods, and of these, the gamma-irradiated variety is the safest. You will find a choice of such foods available, from plankton to krill, brine shrimp, bloodworms and so forth. Try to buy packets that have been carefully handled and not thawed and refrozen, or they may end up as a useless soup.

Dried or freeze-dried forms of many live foods mentioned are also available. They are concentrated and nutritious and are often the best value for the money. Fishes seem to prefer them as they are, although some aquarists soak them before offering them to the fishes to avoid the danger of swelling in the stomach. Offering them sparingly avoids this problem, if it really exists.

Foods processed into flakes or granules offer a mix of different constituents according to requirements, often with added vitamins. Flakes for carnivores or omnivores should contain not less than 45% protein, should float at first, then gradually sink without polluting the water. Those for vegetarians will necessarily have less protein. Color usually means nothing, but some brands are colored according to contents, a useful practice. Granular or pelleted foods are similar to flakes but may contain recognizable pieces of insects, plants, etc., suitable for large fishes. Avoid those that contain low protein contents, intended for coldwater and pond fishes.

OTHER FOODS

Many non-oily canned foods are suitable for marine fishes if chopped to the right size and washed. Crab, lobster, various shellfish, whiting, and squid are examples. Fresh foods from the fishmonger are perhaps best avoided, although I do

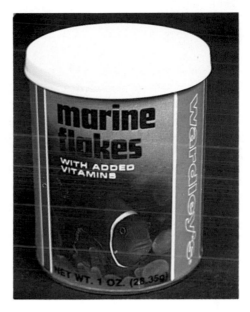

Flake foods that are specially composed to meet the dietary needs of marine fishes are inexpensive and readily available. When feeding flake foods, as with all other food types, never overfeed. Overfeeding quickly leads to cloudy, contaminated water.

not know of any specific instances of trouble arising from their use (they could possibly spread disease). Bread, especially brown bread, is liked by many fishes, and Pacific angels that will not take other dry foods will accept it. Perhaps it looks like a sponge!

INVERTEBRATES

Most crustaceans are no trouble to feed, acting as scavengers of anything that escapes the fishes. Some, particularly crabs, will emerge at night and clean up algae and anything else from the rockwork. Shrimps and lobsters soon learn to steal from anemones, even fishing down into their stomach for pieces of ingested food. If there is any problem about feeding crustaceans because the fishes get it all in the daytime, feed them at night when most of the fishes are resting. Anemones can be fed at this time too, while the crustaceans are busy with their own scraps. The big ones can be taught to accept chunks of food straight into the mouth. First brush it against the tentacles and then place it in the mouth; later it will be accepted without preliminaries.

Filter feeders, such as many anemones, clams, corals, tube worms, and some echinoderms can be fed on newly-hatched brine shrimps, suspensions of mashed-up egg yolk,

liver, brains, and yeast, for example, or on commercially prepared versions of them. Some will even accept very fine dry foods. These suspensions will cloud the water and, if your filters are too vigorous, it is best to turn them off for a short time to give the filter feeders a chance. Just don't forget to turn them on again!

Don't overfeed the filter feeders. As a rough guide, one drop per gallon (4 liters) of concentrated suspension every other day may be enough, particularly in a well-established and well-lit tank that may be producing a significant amount of its own plankton. Some anemones, corals, and other creatures with indwelling algae will also be feeding on the algal products and can in fact grow and flourish without being fed at all by the aquarist. When you first start using invertebrate food in suspended form, it is a good idea to check the nitrate level of the aquarium after, say, a month, and then at intervals to see that it is not rising unduly. If it is, cut down on the feeding of both invertebrates and fishes and give more water changes. If algal growth is not prolific, try to increase it by better illumination and some plant food, obtainable in your pet shop.

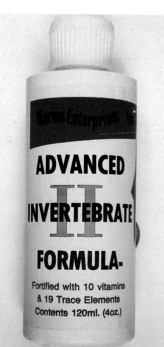

Invertebrates place special feeding demands on the marine aquarist. To the aid of many invertebrate-housing hobbyists come various commercial feeding preparations. Designed to provide for the invertebrates' nutritional needs, these preparations should be given in moderation, not exceeding the recommended dosage.

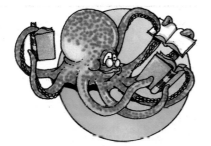

SUGGESTED READING

DR. BURGESS'S ATLAS OF MARINE AQUARIUM FISHES
by Dr. Warren E. Burgess, Dr. Herbert R. Axelrod, Raymond E. Hunziker III
ISBN 0-86622-896-9
TFH H-1100

Contents: Introduction. Aquaristic Section. Caption Explanation. Systematic List of Fish Families. Systematic Pictorial Identification Section.

Audience: Here is a new marine fish book—a truly beautiful and immensely colorful new book—that satisfies the long-existing need for a comprehensive identification guide to marine fishes. This book shows IN FULL COLOR not only the popular aquarium fishes but also the oddballs and weirdos, the large seaquarium type fishes, both warm-water and coldwater fishes, as well as both foreign and domestic fishes.
Hard cover, 8½" × 11", 736 pages, over 4000 full-color photos

MARINE FISHES AND INVERTEBRATES IN YOUR OWN HOME by Dr. Cliff W. Emmens
ISBN 0-86622-790-3 TFH H-1103
Contents: Marine Environment. Some Measurements. Controlling Aquarium Conditions. Biological Filtration. Setting Up Your Marine Aquarium. Buying and Handling Fishes. Feeding Marine Fishes. Diseases and Parasites. The Natural System. Reproduction in Marine Fishes.
Hard cover, 8½" × 11", 192 pages, 315 full-color photos and drawings

HANDBOOK OF FISH DISEASES by Dieter Untergasser
ISBN 0-86622-703-2 TFH TS-123
Contents: Recognizing Diseases. Fish Anatomy. Viral and Bacterial Diseases. Fungal and Algal Diseases. Pathogenic Protozoa. Worm Diseases. Arthropods. Diseases Not Caused by Specific Pathogenic Organisms. Treatment of Diseased Fish.
Hard cover, 8½" × 11", 160 pages, over 100 color photos by the author

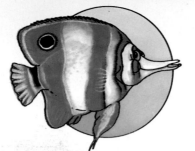

INDEX